GURDJIEFF TODAY

by the same author

Number 1
Transformation of Man Series

J.G. Bennett
GURDJIEFF TODAY

Coombe Springs Press

ISBN 0 900306 17 3
COOMBE SPRINGS PRESS
Sherborne House, Sherborne,
Gloucestershire GL54 3DZ,
England

THE MONOGRAPH SERIES

The Monographs are largely based on lecture talks given by John G. Bennett between October 1971 and December 1974.

Many of the themes and ideas developed in these talks were the foundation for an important series of books which he began writing shortly before his death in December 1974. The aim was to show a new view of the world, an utterly positive one, based on the firm conviction that man must transform himself and that this transformation is to some degree possible for every man and woman. Many of the ideas are taken from Gurdjieff, but have been developed further and sometimes superseded.

John G. Bennett was a mathematician with long experience as a Director of Industrial Research, whose published scientific papers ranged from mathematical physics to the treatment and use of coal.

During the first part of his life he combined his scientific career with research into Asiatic languages and religions and travelled widely in Asiatic countries meeting personally, little known but important spiritual leaders.

Later he gave up his purely scientific work to become Director of the Institute for the Comparative Study of History, Philosophy and the Sciences, where for many years he conducted original research and courses of study directed towards the unification of the major disciplines of science, history, philosophy and religion.

The last years of his life were especially busy establishing the International Academy for Continuous Education at Sherborne House, Sherborne, Gloucestershire, of which he was Principal until his death in December, 1974.

INTRODUCTION

Our work at Sherborne aims at leading us to 'transformation', that is, the unification of the natural and spiritual elements of our being by breaking through the barrier of illusion that keeps them apart. We are aware that mankind is entering a most critical period of history when all will depend upon our ability to respond to the spiritual forces that seek to help us. In this, transformed men and women will be needed as never before in history. Those who feel the truth of this, wish to complete their transformation quickly in order to serve the needs of mankind. For this, all possible means must be employed.

At Sherborne, the work seeks to penetrate to all parts of our nature. By learning practical skills, by taking part in all domestic duties, by working at the Gurdjieff movements and exercises we develop our functions — bodily, emotional and intellectual. By struggling with our negative features we strengthen our will. We also seek to follow Gurdjieff's advice to 'learn ever more and more about the Laws of World Maintenance and World Creation'. More than ever, at the present time, it is necessary for us to seek to understand the world in which we live. It is there that we must work and fulfil the tasks for which we exist as three-brained beings.

We study the world, first through experience and observation, then through books and finally through talks and discussions. Conversation or 'sohbet' is one of the five means by which a Sufi teacher works with his pupils. The true name for a pupil is 'Salik' or seeker, which means seeker of the true. Some have active intellectual powers and a good training, others have a natural, lively curiosity. For them, it is easy to engage in the study of the Laws of World Maintenance and World Creation. Those who lack or imagine they lack, these advantages must have confidence that they can arrive by another route. The Laws are not, in their essence, hard to grasp. They are exemplified in all that we do and in all that happens about us. They can be better grasped in practice than in theory. The scientist or philosopher does not think in terms of universal analogies or cosmic Laws; he may even be repelled by the appearance of ideas which, if only he would entertain them, could revolutionize his understanding of the world.

The present booklet is the first of a series. The text is based on a lecture given at Caxton Hall, London on December, 1973. It is intended for those already acquainted with Gurdjieff's ideas or other Sufi teachings. The same will apply to later booklets. Some of these will similarly discuss a single theme such as Energies, the Laws of Three and Seven, the Second Body of Man, and others will consist of two or three talks on themes proposed week by week for study by the Sherborne students.

If these talks reach the hands of seekers who have no previous knowledge of these ideas and they find them interesting enough to provoke further enquiry, they should write to Coombe Springs Press at Sherborne House, Sherborne, Gloucestershire, England. There are hundreds of groups in many parts of the world who are seeking to prepare themselves for the coming time of troubles. However differently these groups may view the situation and however conflicting their detailed allegiances may appear to be, they need to know one another and share as far as possible their experience and understanding. There is no exclusive way to the truth — no, not even one 'best' way, though each of us may think so. The Work, like Nature, produces a vast multitude of seed and scatters them abroad to ensure that however many may fall by the wayside, the harvest will come at the time of reaping. We must nurture our own seed but not for that neglect the others.

J.G. Bennett, Sherborne 1973.

GURDJIEFF TODAY

Very young children, two or three years old, often begin to ask the question 'Why?' Sometimes they even ask the question 'Why am I here?' Or, if they get the idea of life, they say 'Why am I alive?' Because people do not know how to answer such questions they put them off with foolish answers and soon children stop asking the question 'Why?' Probably they do not grasp the depth and difficulty of the question 'Why?' but that they ask is an indication that somewhere deep down in us this question 'Why?' is there even before we begin to think, even before we are taught anything about ourselves and the world. No one can give a convincing answer, so the question 'Why?' gets gradually covered up and very few people continue to pursue it.

The man about whom I am going to speak tonight, George Gurdjieff, never gave up seeking for the answer to the question 'Why?' This gives him a peculiar significance for our present time. More than ever before we are thrown back upon this question. With Gurdjieff, it never stood still. As time went on, the simple question, 'Why am I alive? took the form of 'Why is there life on the earth? What is this life on earth? In particular, what is our human life? What is its significance, what is it for?' Now this question 'What is our life for?' is much more unusual than you might at first notice. Because generally we have already been put off this question either by being taught that God made us and the world and it is God's business. God alone knows the answer, so it is not our business to inquire. Or else we are told that there is no meaning and purpose to life except what we people bring into it. We are expected to believe that if there are purposes they are all man-made purposes. If this were so the answer to the question 'Why do we exist?' would be: 'To satisfy our own purposes as they arise in us'. The second kind of answer has come to be preferred in the recent centuries and is the one that is still preferred at the present time. Most learned people think that any question about the sense and aim of life must be taken as a man-made question which will have a man-made answer. If so, we can virtually make whatever answer we choose. But if we are not satisfied with that, if we can see that there is something that cannot be right in the belief that the purpose of life on earth is something man-made, then we come up against a new way of looking at the world and life. And it is that new way of looking that makes Gurdjieff's contribution distinctive. If there is a sense and purpose in human life that can be understood, that we have a part to play in fulfilling, and if this applies also to all life, then this purpose must have something to do with this earth, perhaps with this solar system which is the world in which we live. We shall then search for this answer not by going beyond this world altogether, but by looking at the world in a different way. Instead of looking at life on earth as having arisen either through the action of blind causes or by a divine decree coming from outside the world altogether, we shall see it as having come into being, having been designed and organized for purposes that correspond to the size and significance of this solar system within the whole universe. So long as people could think that this earth was the centre of the universe or that our solar system was the central and most important mode of existence in the universe, they could think that all purposes were the same as the purposes of this earth and similar to purposes of man as though he were the highest form of existence on the earth.

One of the most important changes in our view of the world has been due to the discovery that this solar system is a very insignificant item in the great universe. We see now that it would be quite absurd to think that the purposes within the solar system can be the same as those within the universe as a whole. We can say that purposes in the universe are, and are likely to remain, inscrutable to us. But this may not be the case if we are prepared to look at the solar system in itself. Then we have to face quite a new way of looking at the problem of life. If we contemplate a purpose that is neither infinite, transcendental and beyond the universe nor confined to man and his concerns, we are bound to conclude that the purpose is limited and its attainment is hazardous. The history of the earth teaches us that in the course of evolution there have been many promising starts which have failed and left behind them only a few fossils to tell the tale. The human race – Homo sapiens – has one striking example in Neanderthal man who for fifty thousand years tried to establish viable societies and finally failed and disappeared in the arising of a new and more gifted race of men.

The consequences of thinking in terms of a limited, fallible purpose, which is nevertheless far greater than any human purpose, are prodigious. As Gurdjieff said, we may find that we are like sheep and cattle, kept only for their meat, their wool and their hides. It may turn out that man is in the modern phrase – 'an expendible item', whose disappearance might mean a great relief to the earth, a disappointment to the Sun and nothing at all to the rest of the Universe. What matters to us, however, is to learn to live with the idea that there can be purposes which are greater than human purposes and yet are infinitesimal compared with a Universal Purpose. It was this kind of reasoning that led Gurdjieff to ask his question: 'What is the sense and purpose of life on the earth?' When looked at

in the context of the solar system, not in terms of some
Absolute Reality of the universe as a whole, but within
this solar system which we are, to some extent, able to
study and come to terms with, it is necessary to realize
that it calls for a radical change in our way of looking at
our lives. We are forced to think very differently from either
of the two ways which I mentioned just now.

The first answer that Gurdjieff gives to this question:
'What is the sense and purpose of the life on the earth,
and in particular of human life?' comes from looking around
us. Whenever we see that something is being taken care
of on our human level, we expect to be able to answer the
question 'Why are you doing this? What is this for?' When
ever we see human beings taking great care of vast herds
of cattle, flocks of sheep and other animals and we ask
'What are you doing this for?' Is it that you are so fond
of cows and sheep that you feel that you should spend so
much energy in feeding them, preventing them from being
destroyed by predators? The answer is: 'No, no. We are
taking so much care of them because we want their meat,
wool and leather from them'. If we speak in the same way
about mankind, and ask 'What is mankind being preserved
on this earth for?' What should we say? Why was so much
so carefully prepared for mankind over hundreds of millions
of years? Soil that has enabled this vegetation to maintain
life, these various minerals that have been concentrated

under the earth's surface have enabled man to construct all the articles that he uses. Why all this care? Can we examine the question as we did for our sheep and cattle? Can we say: 'It is because some Higher Power is so fond of man that over hundreds of millions of years this state of affairs has been prepared?' Supposing that we give a different answer. 'No, it is not for that reason, it is because something is required from man and this human race, analogous to the requirement that we have for meat, wool and leather'. That is the answer that Gurdjieff came to. It is an answer that has not been in men's minds for a very long time. Probably the last of the great teachers who taught this view of man was Zoroaster and that was 2,500 years ago. It is implicit in the older Jewish scriptures, if one reads them impartially one finds that such an attitude did exist in early biblical times. But now such views have been discarded.

We have such an exalted idea of man that we are not even affronted by the thought that we may, in the eyes of the Higher Powers, be no more than cattle or grass of the field that perishes. We do not even trouble ourselves to contemplate such ridiculous notions that seem to belong to the age of savagery when man was overawed by Nature. Today, man is overawed by nothing except the vision of his own greatness.

Are we to go back to such an ancient view that man

exists here to serve a limited purpose that is not of his own making? Is he here only to be used for something? When these ideas were first introduced to us by Gurdjieff fifty years ago they were very strange; so strange and so shocking that we regarded them as intended only to jolt us, to make us sit up and ask our own question: 'What is my life for? What am I doing with it?' And having received this salutary jolt then to go on living our lives, making use of what we were being taught; but not really facing the implications of the question: 'Are our lives for our own benefit or do we exist to serve some purpose greater than ourselves?' Now, at this present time, a short fifty years since Gurdjieff introduced these notions to the West, it all looks very different. Human purposes are by no means so convincing as they were before. The assumption that man knows what he is doing with his life and that he is making sense of all life on the earth is no longer plausible. We are recklessly destroying life on the earth, we are preparing considerable destruction of human life also. In the last sixty years we have destroyed unnecessarily a great deal of human life. People are very widely beginning to question human purposes and are more ready than they have been for a very long time to look at things in some new way.

Let us now try to unravel the answer to the question that Gurdjieff himself has proposed. It is that human life is required to produce 'something' that is needed for the harmony of the solar system, and particularly for the harmony of this planet and its moon. This 'something' is produced by the way we live our lives and by the way we die our deaths. There is an obligation upon us to produce this 'something' whether we like it or not. This 'something' is analagous to the meat, wool and leather that we get from our sheep and cows.

In the past, people have had the purpose of life presented to them in different ways. But generally speaking, the way of living that has been presented as right for man has been the same. There has been a general understanding of the way that people should live. Apart from certain artificial social customs that have differed from time to time, there has been a general understanding that man is not intended to live for his own egoistic purposes, that he has obligations to fulfil and this is still as true as it has ever been.

Man has understood that he must not live like a wild or rather a mad, animal giving way without restraint to every animal passion and egoistic impulse. He has understood that he must respect his fellow men and accept some kind of social discipline. This pattern of behaviour has been accepted as right and necessary by every kind of society and every variety of culture. What has changed very much over the ages has been the motive that has been put forward to explain why we should live in this way. Let us take a few examples from history. Gautama Buddha appealed to reason. He said: "You see that this life is not satisfying. As it stands it is meaningless. There is only one way out of it and that is to awaken to the Truth, to awaken to Dhamma, this is the Noble Eight-fold Path, to start on the path, you must first accept a disciplined life — or moral code". This appeal to reason was powerful and effective at first, but it changed very soon and lost its power.

Then there was an appeal to faith. This is particularly in the Judaic tradition; we see it in Abraham, Moses and the psalms of David. This is God's command and you believe it. The Jewish scriptures are concerned with strengthening this belief.

The Christian message is that we should base our life upon confidence in the love of God for man and our love for our fellow men. We should live accordingly. Muhammad essentially put forth the doctrine of hope. The Islamic creed is one of hope. The Qu'ran is a message of hope. God is compassionate and makes no demand upon mankind that is too hard to bear. "Fulfil those simple rules of life and salvation is assured". The simple rules correspond to the way of life that is required to fulfil the purpose of our existence.

The Founders of the great religions of the world have

appealed to reason, to faith, to love, to hope. All of them have failed. The appeal to reason does not work. People do not, except for a small minority, live reasonably. Faith has very largely disappeared from the world. It has been replaced by a kind of blind acceptance of what we are told by a conditioning process that is totally different from real faith. The Christian religion has been the most tragical failure of all. In the name of love more wickedness and cruelty have been perpetrated than by the followers of any other religion. Because Islam is newer than the others it is perhaps the last to evaporate, but this religion of hope also is being replaced by motives that are totally different from those put forward by Muhammad the Founder. In short, the ways in which men have been directed towards a way of living that corresponds to our obligations on this earth have all failed.

Modern man has invented a new reason, that is: self-interest. We shall live in a certain way because it is more satisfying. We are less likely to get into trouble, we are more likely to have a 'good life' if we live more or less in the same way as people have always been taught to live. The religion of self-interest is the newest of all. It rejects any other motive for right living except self-interest. But it is also the one that has collapsed the most rapidly. We are already seeing the tragical consequences of the religion of self-interest.

All of this is a paraphrase of Gurdjieff's presentation
of the situation in his own books. With what does he come
forward as an alternative to these ways? He says that
it is necessary now for man to begin to see things as they
really are. We have in us an instrument that enables us
to see the truth, not indirectly through what other people
have taught us but by a direct perception. The instrument
of this direct perception he calls by the ancient name of
'conscience'. So far I have not spoken about the 'something' that man has to provide by his way of life. Now
we have come to Gurdjieff's message, which is, in effect,
'It is time for man to see for himself why he should live
in a certain way. We must ourselves see what our lives
are for, **what is the sense and significance of our existence'**.

We have come to a moment of maturing in human life,
when we have to pass out of a childish dependence upon
what others tell us and be able to see for ourselves. It is
a very difficult moment for us when as individuals we have
to 'grow up'. It is very much more difficult as applied to the
human race as a whole. Maybe it will take centuries before
we can come to it. But we are at a moment of transition
when we have to learn to look at life differently. Not in
terms of what has been taught and believed in the past,
but in terms of what we ourselves are able to see, to experience by our own direct perceptions in the present. In

order to see, one must recognize what one is looking at. Therefore some indication has to be given.

What I am now about to say is one of the most extraordinary steps in Gurdjieff's presentation. I am not aware of it having been taught before nor that it is being taught at the present time in any other tradition. There are indications as I said before, that it was taught by Zoroaster, that remarkable prophet of whom we know so little, and probably by Pythagoras who according to tradition was taught by Zoroaster himself. It is not really important that it was known to a few people in the remote past but what does matter is that it should be known now and that we should be able to see it for ourselves. Gurdjieff calls it the **Doctrine of Reciprocal Maintenance.** This doctrine of reciprocal maintenance is that everything that exists in the universe depends on other things for its maintenance and must in its turn maintain the existence of others. He adds that this applies to us men also. It is very easy to see that we depend on other forms of existence. We depend on the materials of this earth's surface, upon the heat and light that come from the sun and upon other things that we do not know about. But most of all, we depend upon **life.** We are an integral part of the life of this earth and we cannot isolate ourselves from it. We could not eat and in truth we could not breathe without life on the earth, because it is the life on the earth that supplies the oxygen which makes it possible for us to breathe. Then the question comes 'If we depend upon so much for our existence, what have we got to give in return? What is required of us?'

It is not enough to say that our bodies will return to the earth, because we are a great deal more than living organisms. We cannot say that our debt to life will be paid simply by returning our carcass to the earth from which it came. What have we more? We share with all life the property of sensitivity. This sensitivity is more highly organized in us than in any other form of life. We are capable of more varied experiences. These experiences cannot be for nothing; they are not given to us for our own pleasure and suffering. Human experience releases energies which could not be produced in any other way. To explain this in detail would take much more time then there is available tonight. Let us assume that we do recognize that human experience is different from any other form of experience on this earth. If all experience is associated with some kind of sensitive energy, then we are all producing energy according to the kind of experience we have – which in turn depends upon the way in which our lives are lived – we shall produce energies of different qualities. Gurdjieff asserts that certain of these are the very 'something' that is required for the orderly evolution of this solar system. A great process of sensitization, or as he calls it, of spiritualization, is proceeding on this earth and throughout the solar system, and we have to make our contribution to it. And we must do so by the way in which we live our lives.

We know that we take a great deal from this earth. We are beginning to see that we are taking more than we are entitled to, that we are running heavily into debt towards the earth and towards life. This makes it even more important for us to know how to repay, how to square our account with the earth and with life. We are forced to admit that we are running into bankruptcy as a human race with debts that we shall scarcely be able to repay. This is somehow felt by people all over the world and makes them very uneasy about the way things are going in human societies. We can interpret all this in ordinary terms, of exhaustion of resources and pollution and all the other things that we know about. Deeper down there is something that we suggest by such phrases as 'rape of the earth', 'destruction of our environment'. These make us deeply uneasy but we do not understand the full significance of it all. We may readily imagine that there are Higher Intelligences who are surveying human life and know that it is possible for man to live otherwise. Gurdjieff assures us that the Higher Powers are deeply concerned that man should live otherwise, but that they are dependent upon human understanding for this change to come about. If it is true that we people do not exist on the earth to please ourselves, or just by accident, but because we are needed for a purpose that is greater than ourselves; it must follow that, if we totally fail to fulfil this purpose, we shall be removed and replaced by some other form of life.

These things that I am saying may not be as explicit as this in your mind, but I think that most of you have some feeling that there is something wrong with our present attitude towards life on the earth and towards human life in particular. There is something seriously missing in our understanding of human destiny. Therefore we should look very seriously at the answer that Gurdjieff gives.

There is a missing link. We are not seeing that our lives are required for 'something'. If we provide that 'something' our lives will have fulfilled their purpose and we will be set free from our debt. Our own individual fulfilment will then be made possible. This cannot be in isolation, separately from the rest of mankind, as people have sometimes thought in the past. In olden days, it was supposed that the quest for a higher and a more significant life was a private matter, that every man could pursue for himself, in solitude if need be. They thought that we should seek the company of other people only if we need them to teach us or if we feel stronger because we are sharing with others. Such individualistic — and indeed egoistic — views no longer hold water. There is something here in which the whole of the human race is involved. We not only need

one another, but we have an underlying connection by
this very fact that the whole of the human race is needed
for a certain purpose. If it fulfils this purpose this human
race of ours has the possibility of moving to a very different level of fulfilment, where a new significance can
enter human life.

It is this that represents the attraction of the New World.
There is a possibility for man to come to a different, differently satisfying life, providing only that people can
see that this obligation of ours to provide that certain
'something' is fulfilled. Then comes the question of how
this is to be done. What has Gurdjieff to say about this?
In general, there is a great difference between **knowing
what** and **knowing how**. At this moment the truth is that
people neither know what, nor how, to live. They only
feel that there is a way in which they should live but
not why they should follow this way. They see, if they
are at all sensible, impartial and honest with themselves
that they are not living as they should. There is something
wrong with our own behaviour which is not something
we can unload on to other people. We need to know how
to live our lives differently, but the first thing is to know
what is this 'differently'. Just to live a moral well-ordered
life is not enough. We need consciously to fulfil the obligation to produce the special energies that are required
from us.

The 'How' Gurdjieff calls **conscious labour and intentional suffering**. This phrase appears again and again in all his writings. It is necessary to understand just what he means by it. Conscious labour is nearly the same as what we should call **service**. It is to serve the purpose of our existence, and this is very much concerned with the future of mankind. Throughout his own life and in every picture that he drew in his own books of the way in which life should be lived he always emphasised the obligation we have to serve the **Future**: to 'prepare a better future for mankind'. We must learn to make present sacrifices for the sake of the future.

As parents, we all see and recognize the necessity to make present sacrifices for our own children's futures. This is true, but too limited. Apart from recognition of our obligations as parents, how little remains that we are prepared to do and to sacrifice for the future. How little we are ready to do without things now, to place restraints upon our desires and impulses of the present, in order that a better future should be possible. How little do we recognize that power is not to be exercised in order to get what we want now but in order to serve the future. It is round such things as these that the meaning of 'conscious labour' is to be understood. Why is it **conscious** labour? Because it is necessary to know what has to be done. It is an exceedingly difficult thing to serve the future rightly. Many people want to do good for the future but they do not know what is needed. They do not know how to sow the seeds that will make a better future.

We need a change of our perceptions. Something needs to be understood that is not now understood. One of the things that has to be understood is that right living will always involve payment and sacrifice. It is not fashionable nowadays to accept the necessity for suffering because we do not wish to admit the necessity to suffer if we are to serve. We are reluctant to give, even from our abundance. How much less when it actually hurts us. There are people I know – some of whom are in this room – who live their lives prepared to put themselves in situations where they will have to suffer in order to be of service to other people. They know that this suffering will be inevitable.

It is not enough to have the good will to serve and suffer, it is also necessary to have new kinds of perceptions, a new understanding of other people, otherwise we are liable to blunder. With the best intentions we can do harm and not good to other people, sow evil and not good seeds for the future. Therefore we have also the obligation to understand human life better. This understanding starts with the understanding of what human life is for. A great part of Gurdjieff's teaching was concerned with the study and understanding of man. Not just as a being to live successfully on this earth, but essentially as a being who has obligations to fulfil and who, through fulfilling these obligations, can fulfil himself. This is the notion of the **transformation of man**. Through this, people come together. In the absence of this, people are separated. Our present life suffers terribly from isolation and loneliness. There is the disintegration of family life which is one of the symptoms. But in general it is one of the sad features of our great cities that there is so much less understanding and connection between people than in the past. Our great organizations have become so impersonal that the very core of human existence is dropping away. That core is the sense of the **unity of mankind**.

We have to move towards this unity not as it was understood in the past, but in new ways. There will be changes. Something will emerge and is beginning to emerge now, in the form of new perceptions, the ability for people to communicate without words and without outward signs, through a deeper understanding and perception of one another. There is a term that is commonly used, but it is very important to use it rightly: that is the term **Group-consciousness**. It is used now because people are aware that in some way or other we have to get beyond our isolated and separated individualities, to the awareness of the connection between us. I said that life by reason, life by faith, life by love and hope have all failed; so something else, a new kind of perception must come that

will restore these sacred qualities to their real significance in human life. We must be very careful that we do
not in the same way spoil and lose the real significance
of the emerging 'group-consciousness'. There is a very
great risk that as the ideas that belong to the New World
begin to emerge, people will take them in old ways and
not see that we have to move to something quite new and
different.

There is indeed such a thing as group-consciousness.
I have experienced it with many people and we have begun
to know what this really can be. We know that this is one
of the new modes that will enter the New World. Group-
consciousness comes through the transformation of energies
that are required from man and will make us very much
more effective in the fulfilment of our obligations. I have
spoken of the need to take a conscious part in the reciprocal maintenance of everything in this solar system.
All this will be made more effective through group-consciousness. The most important of all is that we should
be able to perceive directly, not by what other people have
told us but through the development of a new consciousness
within ourselves. We should be able to see directly what
the purpose of our life is, how everything is connected,
how life is not separated from life, how it must be served,
and how the fulfilment of our own destiny comes in doing
that.

These things have been taught to us before in the form
of moral rules. This is the way children are taught. 'This
is what you ought to do'. 'This is what your father tells
you to do'. We have to go past that and see for ourselves.
Here again Gurdjieff made an enormous contribution by
his long years of search through different countries of
the world where he was able to come into contact with
ancient groups that had at some time found and preserved
the secret of this transformation of consciousness. He
even saw how to develop a different kind of group awareness and to overcome the defects of our human nature.
He left these techniques behind him when he died. His
contribution was not only to tell what the New World will
be like, but also not a little about how it can be brought
about.

I have spoken up till now in terms of what Gurdjieff
taught because this lecture is about him. You may feel
that I have exaggerated his importance. It is not in terms
of importance that I speak, but in terms of the uniqueness
and the unexpectedness of his message. If you set yourself
to understand this message more closely, you will see
that there is something really strange that this should
be so different from so much that is being said at the
present time. There are so many people proclaiming the
advent of the New World and telling us what man should
do about it. They speak justly and rightly about new forms

of consciousness and new perceptions, but they overlook this particular fact that our life must be governed by the obligation to produce something needed for the world. Since this is connected with the way we experience, it follows that we must transform our own way of life. This is something I do not see elsewhere. Many other valuable things are being said and done that are all necessary and contribute to making the new world but this particular teaching is the most important of all. Why is this? Because we are now coming to the point where we people have to understand what our lives are for. It is no longer enough to do what we are told nor live by the promise of something wonderful for ourselves if we do what we are told. We have to be more mature than that.

I will finish my lecture at this point and ask you if there are any things about which you would like me to speak more fully.

—

Question: What does Gurdjieff mean by Conscious Labour and Intentional Suffering? How do they apply to what you have been saying?

J. G. B.: It is a good question which goes to the root of the matter. I said that we have to serve the future. The simplest possible example is the relation of parent and child. When parents truly fulfil their obligations towards their children they take on conscious labour and intentional suffering. Unless they are complete fools they know that they will have to work and suffer. No parent who loves his children has ever not suffered. We must accept this suffering and know that our relation with our children must be one of giving and not of demanding. We must know we have to sacrifice our own self-love. We must not expect something in return from our children and at the same time we must not avoid the suffering that will come to us through being firm with our children. It is a very hard discipline to be a good parent. That is a characteristic example of conscious labour and intentional suffering.

It requires a great deal of understanding. One cannot be a good parent merely by wanting to. However much one may love one's children one will make mistakes unless one has set oneself to understand; to be able to enter into their experience. This is why conscious labour and intentional suffering requires a change of perception.

Question: What do you think about Gurdjieff as a man? Was he as white or as black as he is painted? What was he trying to do with all his strange behaviour? You had personal contact with him, what did you make of him?

J.G.B.: I have just written a book about Gurdjieff; as I decided to write this about him I set myself to answer that question in 364 pages. But let me try to give a short answer to it. Gurdjieff had an exceptionally hard life and this was largely due to his own exceptionally difficult nature. He had a great deal to overcome in himself. He had extraordinary powers which he very seldom exercised because for certain reasons he knew that he had to refrain from exercising them. It is quite true I have had personal contact with him. I have seen that he had powers that were not ordinary, not like anyone else I have personally met. He could have lived a very comfortable life if he had chosen to make use of his powers. But on the contrary he led throughout an extremely difficult life. He was concerned from quite an early age, from the age of thirty-two onwards, in seeing how he could transmit to people what he himself had been fortunate enough to learn. From 1909 to 1949, that is forty years, he laboured to find ways of transmitting, constantly experimenting, sometimes making quite serious mistakes, but never ceasing to search right to the end of his life for ways in which he could transmit to people the things that he had been able to learn through exceptionally favourable circumstances.

You must understand that he made a distinction between intentional suffering and voluntary suffering. Sometimes one can voluntarily inflict suffering on oneself in order to gain a particular result for one's benefit. An athlete will inflict suffering upon himself, undergoing severe training and exert a great deal of self-control in order to develop his powers as an athlete. Such voluntary suffering is quite different from intentional suffering. **Intentional suffering is accepting the consequences of actions one undertakes for the benefit of others.** Anyone who sincerely wishes to do something for the benefit of others must understand that this will always bring trouble on himself. It is a law that Gurdjieff understood very well. He brought a great deal of trouble on himself. Intentional suffering simply means that one accepts the consequences of one's actions, knowing that this will include painful experiences. Voluntary suffering is different. Here one is doing something for a definite purpose, in general, for one's own benefit, as a miser will starve to fill his coffer.

Question: Gurdjieff's ideas have so far received little public support. Do you think that this will change? Do you see him as a prophet of the New Age?

J. G. B.: He was certainly a precursor who saw far more clearly than most people of his time that there was something terribly wrong with the way people were living and behaving all over the world. As I read the present situation twenty-five years after Gurdjieff died, the time has come when it is possible to put much more effectually into practice what he taught than has been the case hitherto. That is one reason why I am speaking as I am now. In the last two or three years, I have been making an experiment on these lines myself with a number of people at Sherborne House. I want to talk to you about that because it is an experiment following a plan Gurdjieff himself indicated in the organization of his own Institute some fifty years ago. It is for training people on the lines I have been speaking of: that is, in the development of their powers of perception both external and internal, and in showing them how it is possible to come to group-consciousness. That is a big undertaking and I can only attempt it with people who are able and prepared to devote themselves entirely to it for a fairly long period of time. For various reasons I decided that it needs **ten months** time. I am looking for people who have the potential for developing these powers because it is very important that those who have this potential should be prepared as soon as possible. There is a growing need for people who have this capacity.

That is the task that I have set myself at Sherborne. I have been working also with a number of people in the London area, as far as possible on the same lines but without the intensive conditions. It is not possible in the short time available to tell you more than the general principles of what Gurdjieff presents to us as the way in which the New World will come about. I regard it as my duty to share with people as far as is possible for me what I myself have learned from Gurdjieff and other teachers.

Question: What is the meaning of the picture behind you with the words **"Is There 'Life' on the Earth?"**?

J.G.B.: It is the title of a book just published in America. I asked Gerald Wilde, an artist who is living with us at Sherborne, a man of extraordinary genius, to draw me something for tonight which would ask the question: "Is there 'Life' on the earth?" This is what he drew. It must speak for itself.

Question: What happens to people who begin to work on themselves and then give up the struggle? Isn't it worse for them than if they had never started?

J. G. B. : I have long experience. It is more than fifty years since I first met Gurdjieff and Ouspensky, I have seen people over the greater part of their lives. I have seen people who started and appeared to have given up. Very often I later have seen that it was not true that it was worse for them. I am talking now from actual experience and observation. If something has really started in people they may give up outwardly but something continues beneath the surface. Maybe many years later one sees that the process has not stopped in them.

In the last year of Gurdjieff's life I remember very well a man that I had known who was the first Englishman that ever met Gurdjieff in the Caucasus just before he came to Constantinople where I first met him in 1920. He was a very good Russian scholar and very valuable to Gurdjieff as a translator. He was very close to Gurdjieff in the early years, but after a certain time he appeared to drop out. Things went very badly with him. But he came over to Paris in 1949 to see Mr. Gurdjieff. I was sitting on one side of Mr. Gurdjieff and he was sitting on the other and he asked him: "I have given up, is it too late for me to start again?" Gurdjieff said: "It is never too late. This work does not stop. If you will follow my indications now, you will find what you are looking for before you die". It was an unforgettable moment because this spanned a whole lifetime. He did indeed die well. I have seen this more than once in my long experience. People who have apparently given up have not lost the inner working. If there is in people a genuine longing to discover the true significance of life, they may give up for external or for personality reasons, but once the seed is sown, it must continue to mature. Of course, if the contact with it was fictitious or mental only, it is another matter. If they never did anything but pretend then no seed has been sown. Those who really give up are the ones who never started In telling you this, I am not quoting from anyone else's books or teachings. I am talking of my own personal experience.

Question: Can you tell us if Gurdjieff expected a world catastrophe? Did he prepare for what was going to happen? Did he foresee a great fight between the powers of good and evil?

J.G.B.: I do not think he expected the wholesale destruction of a great part of the human race. The end of the old world and the start of the new was the subject of the very last talk I had with him just a week almost to the hour before he died. I was with him for two hours that Saturday morning, 22nd October, 1949, and he was speaking about the conflict between the old world and the new. He referred to this very confrontation you have in mind, of open conflict between the East and the West, as he put it, which at that time was apparently imminent between the U.S.A. and the U.S.S.R. He said, "This looks unavoidable but it will not happen. This is not the real conflict which is between the old world and the new. It is not between one form of materialism and another form of materialsim. This real conflict between the old and new", he said, "is a serious one. The outcome is not guaranteed. It is not possible for the world to be 'made tchic'". He clearly identified himself with the New World when he said: "Either I will make the old world 'tchic' or it will make me 'tchic'. Now another great war will not happen. When Beelzebub is published a new force will come into the world".

I think we have to take into account that there is an enormous inertia in the old world whose death we are witnessing today. In another talk I gave on this subject I spoke about dinosaurs. A hundred million years ago, life on earth was dominated by the reptiles which reached enormous sizes. The dinosaurs were huge, small-brained, slow-moving creatures who were well adapted to the mild and stable climates of the Cretaceous Period. When the world climate changed, that dominant form of life gave up and was replaced by much more active and positive forms of life. We are at the present moment in a **dinosaur civilization.** Enormous, slow-moving, small-brained organizations are now dominating the world. The dinosaurs gradually lost as the climate became too inhospitable for them. They became more and more helpless and a new form of life emerged: that is, the warm-blooded mammals. This is extraordinarily like the present situation in the world. We are, at the present moment, dominated by large organizations, governments, churches, industrial giants, financial groups, international organizations. All these are large and they grow larger as the dinosaurs did. It is visible to everyone that their level of intelligence and their ability to look into the future are exceedingly small. They are quite unable to adapt to the New World but they will not give up easily. They are unable to adapt to the new climate; the climate for these big organizations was that of expansion. As long as there was room and the means to expand they could thrive. This climate is changing and we are entering a period when it no longer will be possible to expand. Growth will be impossible. Then it will be not merely a duty but a necessity to control, to restrain and concentrate. Under such circumstances, big organizations collapse. They can only exist in a state of expansion. This we can see. It is possible to explain just why it must be so. But this is not necessary because we can see it for ourselves.

The New World will be dominated by active, mobile and much more intelligent forms of social life. This is why we have to look to small groups and communities; and above all to the emergence of **group-consciousness** which corresponds to the state of the warm-blooded animals. We need a warm-blooded society, not the present cold-blooded society. Because of the great advantage warm blood has over cold in times of stress, I believe that the New World will survive. There will be a time of great difficulties, and it is not desirable that the collapse of the old world should come suddenly. It would probably not be possible to survive a sudden collapse of order throughout the world. Little by little the old world will die out. New social forms, new modes of existence will take its place. For this, we must prepare ourselves today. If we have a feeling towards that, if something in us responds to that, then our first duty is to prepare.

Question: Do you see a connection between what you have been saying and the work you are doing at Sherborne House?

J.G.B.: Indeed I do, a very close relationship.

Question: How is true group-consciousness achieved?

J.G.B.: It is necessary to pass through certain experiences together. But as I have said before there is fictitious group-consciousness and there is real group-consciousness. To understand the difference is very important for anyone who is concerned about the society of the future. It is possible to produce an emotional excitement shared by a large number of people. This is not 'group-consciousness' but 'crowd-consciousness'. It is quite different and really the opposite. Crowd-consciousness is always wasteful even if it is not destructive. Group-consciousness is always creative. Crowd-consciousness can be produced by external stimulus whereas group-consciousness can only be achieved by internal change.

What we have at Sherborne House is a school modelled as far as possible on what Gurdjieff prescribed when he was laying down the organization of his own Institute for the Harmonious Development of Man. The aim is precisely that: the harmonious development of all sides of our nature. This means not only our intellectual, bodily and emotional powers but also to develop the will which is 'I', the spiritual nature of man. For this, we have very varied activities. All kinds of skills are learned, everything is done in common. All the people living at Sherborne — there are about a hundred and twenty altogether — work together and go through this training. The practical skills include the work of the house, care of animals, food production, carpentry, stone masonry and many other arts and crafts. The rapid learning of new skills, especially when they are learned by people working together in groups, develops perceptions and common understanding, thus preparing the ground for group-consciousness.

We make a great deal of use of the extraordinary discoveries of Gurdjieff in the field of bodily exercises, including sacred dances and rituals. We also work on various psychological, historical and philosophical questions. We study language, art and music so that as far as possible all sides of our nature are developed together. Ages range from 18 to 70 and the students come from ten to fifteen countries although the majority are Americans. You can read about it in the Prospectus of the Academy. It is called the International Academy for Continuous Education to emphasize that it has an international character, and that it is for the all round development of man. This is the idea of the Academy and it is something for our entire lives. We do not look upon education as something one does once and for all in one's youth; but that the process of our harmonious development must continue, as Gurdjieff put it, until our 'last breath'.

Sherborne is for me the fulfilment of something that Gurdjieff spoke to me about in August, 1923. He told me many things about his plans and how he hoped his Institute would develop. I was particularly fortunate because I could speak Turkish nearly as well as English. Gurdjieff could talk Turkish perfectly because it was the lingua franca of the part of the world where he grew up. I was able to talk more with him than most visitors so that I was able to learn from him all that he chose to tell me about his ideas for the future. These have remained with me and it was an extraordinary opportunity that came only about three years ago to be able to put a great deal of that into practice and see how it worked. It is remarkable to see how well he foresaw so long ago what would be needed. He did say that this would come in the future.

Question: Can you tell me more about Gurdjieff and his life. I have read many of the books but have the impression that we have not heard the whole story. Why did his Institute not continue and develop at that time?

J. G. B.: Ostensibly, Gurdjieff's Institute for the Harmonious Development of Man folded up owing to an almost fatal motor accident in July, 1924. You must realize that he was at an enormous disadvantage; because, although he spoke many Eastern languages, at that time he could hardly speak any European language. He depended upon interpreters. When, in addition, he was nearly killed by this frightful accident, he just could not continue. He was forced to abandon all his plans for the Institute, and instead put his ideas in writing. That is how his books came to be written. There were also deeper reasons that Gurdjieff discloses in the Third Series of his writings.

Question: Can you tell us how your work and that of Idries Shah are connected. Is he interested in Sherborne House?

J.G.B.: Shah has his work to do and I have mine. They are different and scarcely overlap at all. Shah is stirring people up very effectively all over the world. He is making them think, showing them that modes of thought that appear to be free are really psychologically conditioned. He has the cooperation and support of scholars, scientists and men of action all over the world. He is doing a very important work on a much larger scale than anything that I am attempting. It aims at awakening people to the absurdity and also the gravity of the present situation and of giving people hope of a way out. It is a direct action that concerns the immediate future of mankind. I said to somebody today that I regard Shah as the Krishnamurti of Sufism. As Krishnamurti goes about breaking down people's fixed ideas, so is Shah doing a good deal to break down people's illusions. This is a very necessary preparation for the New World.

What I am trying to do is to take people who have enough determination and aptitude to go through a fairly rigorous training and prepare themselves to serve the world in its process of transformation. So that my task is a quite different one; it is directed to a more distant future of ten, twenty or even fifty years hence.

Question: It seems to me that what you are saying is very close to what Idries Shah and the Sufis are saying.

J. G. B.: It is very close. A great part of Gurdjieff's ideas came from Sufi sources. But I think you will see that this particular thing that I have been talking about today is not to be found in any Sufi literature you know about. There is another, probably more ancient, tradition alongside the Sufi tradition in which this knowledge was transmitted. It is known as the Sarman Brotherhood. It was not until Gurdjieff found this Sarman tradition that he really saw the answer to his question, 'What is the sense and significance of human life?' You must understand that Sufi Tradition is a broad term. If we speak of the 'Christian Tradition' we know that we have to make an important distinction between Eastern and Western Christianity. It is not only a matter of doctrine, but of the way in which the spiritual life is understood in the East and the West. There are also great differences in Islam and particularly in Sufism. Whereas Islamic doctrine tells the believer what he must do; Sufism tells him how to do it. In my personal opinion, after long years of study and having met many Sufis in many parts of the world, the core of Sufi tradition comes from Central Asia. There is a very ancient source from which many traditions have originated: Vedic, Avestan or Zoroastrian, Buddhist, Mithraic, and much of Judaism and Christianity. Before Sufism entered Islam, Buddhism was the dominant tradition in Central Asia. That is why the true Central Asian Sufism is as much Buddhist as it is Islamic.

Question: You speak about the possibility of acquiring new perceptions. Where does this power come from? How could I know whether I have it or not?

J.G.B.: All people have it. That is how man is made. We are endowed with this possibility just as much as we are with the possibility of touching and smelling and seeing, indeed, more so, because one can be born blind, but one is not born without this possibility. It is inherent in the very essence of human nature but that does not mean that everyone has an equal chance of achieving it. Not at all. That may vary greatly between one person and another. How far people can go also varies enormously. Those who are able to go all the way are the rarest of the rare. That is how it is arranged. But everyone has the potential to realize or neglect, it is a matter of our own choice. That is said in the new law of Moses: "Behold I set before you this day life and death, blessing and cursing, choose therefore life that thou and thy seed may live". I am personally concerned, my task is to find people who have a high potential and help them to realize it. That does not mean that there is not much to be done for everyone but if people who have a high potential will be prepared to accept 'conscious labour and intentional suffering', they can then become the means of help to many others beside themselves. This is really the principle: if you are able to receive much you are also able to give much.

Question: Do people who go to Sherborne all get this?

J. G. B.: This is now beginning to emerge. The people who came in the first year in 1971 have now been able to see what they are able to do. I myself am very satisfied. By no means all of them could continue independently but a certain number are able to and are at this present time able to share with others something of what they received during their Basic Course.

This is happening in different parts of the world. In all this you must understand that I have been guided by the pattern which Gurdjieff laid down. He intended that people who went through a training at his central institute should afterwards be able to go to different places and pass on what they had received.

Question: Is there a chance of saving the world from disaster?

J. G. B.: The old world is past saving. During this present century the first great disaster has already occurred. This was due to the failure of mankind to recognize the enormous responsibility we incurred through our great technical discoveries, especially the release of energy through steam, internal combustion engines and electrical generators. This release of energy threw the world out of balance. Only conscious people could have rectified it. According to Gurdjieff, there was a group in Tibet who could have saved the world, but their leader was killed by a stray bullet when the British invaded Tibet in 1902 and the rest of the group died soon after. This group knew the secret of generating the spiritual energies needed to neutralize the destructive forces released by our technical discoveries. Gurdjieff had learned a part of this secret and passed it on to us. It is the answer to his question 'What is the sense and significance of human life on this earth'?

Because of the disaster in 1902, the world collapsed. Two world wars and the loss of forty million lives were the visible consequences. The breakdown of human societies and the threat of a third world war were before us in 1950 but strange things happened that averted the final tragedy.

Now we must think of saving the New World. We continue to make technical discoveries and release more and more energy. If we succeed in harnessing the energy of atomic fusion a really frightful situation will arise. The work started in Tibet a hundred years ago will have to be resumed on a far greater scale.

To save the world three different kinds of action are required: one is visible and two are invisible. The visible work is to prepare the new social order. We shall need 'work communities' or, as Gurdjieff called them, 'Fourth Way Schools'. These will be devoted to training people to survive and perfect themselves under the severe conditions of the next hundred years. These schools will have the practical task of creating self-supporting communities able to work together and share resources and also to help their environment. This is much harder than it looks.

Modern man is a taker and not a giver. Whoever has power uses it to take and hold, whereas the only right use of power is to give and share with others. It is possible to go far enough in the elimination of egoistic grasping after one's own benefit to be able to live and work in a community. But this requires teaching and training. That is what Fourth Way Schools are for; but only on the exoteric or outer plane.

The deeper, mesoteric work is concerned with energies. Psychic and spiritual energies must be released, concentrated, stored up and put to work in the right way. This requires very special knowledge and readiness to work and sacrifice. There are schools in the world that are doing this today but they are not in the West. We need to take up this work ourselves.

If people are willing to undertake such work, they must first be tested to see if they have the required qualities. They must be able to put aside personal ambition and set themselves to serve the future without expectation of reward. Gurdjieff once said that 200 conscious people could stop war. If this number will be available by 1990, the disaster that threatens mankind will be averted.

At Sherborne, we have made a start and already a few people are on the way. In 1977, I hope to have a special course for those who have prepared themselves. If all goes well we shall contribute our quota to the group of energy transformers. There are other centres where similar preparations are going on.

Finally, there is the true esoteric work that is supernatural. There is at this present time a great spiritualizing action that is preparing the New Epoch. This action comes, as Gurdjieff puts it, 'from Above'. All we can do is to cooperate with it and be its instruments. The Spirit cannot work without the Flesh. The New World communities are the flesh of the new humanity. Spiritual energies are its blood but its life is entering from Above.

I have confidence that this action will succeed and that many of you here today will see the birth of the New World.

~

The Transformation of Man Series

by John G. Bennett

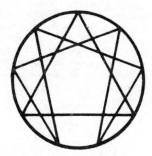

These Monographs present a new view of the world — an utterly positive one.

They are based on the firm conviction that man must transform himself — and that this transformation is to some degree possible for every man and woman.

Many of the ideas are founded on the work of Gurdjieff, but in these lecture talks given between 1971 and 1974 Mr Bennett developed on Gurdjieff's teachings and sometimes superseded them.

Gurdjieff Today ①

This Monograph is the first of a series, *The Trans-formation of Man*. The text is based on a lecture given at Caxton Hall London in December 1973. It is intended, as are all the Monograph series, for those already acquainted with Gurdjieff's ideas or other Sufi teachings.

When Gurdjieff first came to France and introduced his system of psychological techniques, the significance of his ideas and methods were not widely acknowledged

Now, some fifty years later, as we find ourselves in an increasingly chaotic world, the relevance of his system is being seen by more and more people who seek a meaning for their existence. It is in that that Gurdjieff's system is distinctive for he emphasises that we have "to look at this world differently" and gives us the methods and tecniques to do so.

ISBN 0 900306 13 0

The Enneagram ②

The Enneagram is an ancient symbol of profound significance. The understanding of its use has been passed down through hidden spiritual brother-hoods for well over 2,000 years. During his travels in search of teachers of wisdom Gurdjieff found the Enneagram used as a method of passing on traditional teachings.

Since his first contact with Gurdjieff, Mr Bennett studied and used the Enneagram for fifty years and was a well qualified exponent of its mysteries. Using everyday situations to illustrate its workings as well as showing its deeper significance, Bennett reveals possibilities for coming to an understanding of the underlying principles of the laws of the universe.

ISBN 0 900306 17 3

Sex ③

That sex is important in human life is obvious, but
in all that has been written about it there are only
partial glimpses of what it means. One person looks
upon sex as a physiological phenomenon, another
as a force in society. Or one will wish to understand what is required for parenthood, while
another is interested in the idea of 'the trans-
mutation of sex energy'. In taking these partial
views, the whole is lost, and cannot be understood.
In this Monograph an attempt is made to explain
the nature of the sexual act and what 'right sexual
activity' could mean. Sex is looked at in terms of
its influence on creativity and perception; the
structure and origins of parenthood and the con-
dition of marriage or true union. The Monograph
ends with a sketch of a sane society in which
sex could find its rightful place.

ISBN 0 900306 16 5

The Sevenfold Work ④

The Work requi~ ̤s that we try to understand how
to work and what the Work is for. At the very least
it is an action that takes us out of the mechanical
stream of events, that demands of us more than
animal survival. There are techniques to be learned
ideas to be assimilated and various modes of action
to be practised, but the work is evolutionary and
no static set of precepts and exercises can be
enough.

In this Monograph the Work is resolved into a
spectrum of seven lines-Assimilation, Struggle,
Service, Manifestation, Receptivity, Submission,
Purity-a truly balanced Work, and what belongs to
each of the seven lines. It is based on material
from talks and discussions held at Sherborne
House during 1974.

ISBN 0 90036 23 8

The Image of God in Work ⑤

Every image that we can have of God turns out to be inadequate. God as a personal being is too much like us to be the creator of the world containing us. God as a totally impersonal force is too remote to enter into the meeting with us in which every praying man believes.

Those who 'pray of God' are not totally deluded. There is an action in this prayer which is objective.What is it that enables there to be prayer at all and how is it that it can be effective? The answer to this lies in the extraordinary nature of *sacred images*. They are the bridge between man and God, between this world and a higher one. They have been created to be just that and their origin is in an invisible event initiated from a higher world. The experiencings, thoughts and sufferings of countless people blend with something 'from Above' to make the image with power to help. The image is truly God in that it is a channel for the Compassion that comes to redeem us from the consequences of the past.

Mr Bennett, in these talks shows that it cannot be right to think of God as a being. He distinguishes between the creative intelligence that fashions the world and the Divine Love that makes it real. Yet, there is no attempt to suggest that these examinations provide what is needed - a new sacred image. The image can arise only from an action initiated from Above. All we can do is prepare. We can clear away some of the confusion. We can find the reality of higher intelligence and God in our work.We, even we ordinary people, can, through the Work, really know God.

What is to come we cannot even guess at. Mr Bennett hints at the special role that a heightened awareness of Nature might play, but we can only pray and worship as we find it possible. If we take our thinking to the limit we can come to accept the authenticity of the prayer of the simple man. If we give ourselves to the Work we can taste the reality of God and strive to prepare for the Incarnation that is to come.

ISBN 0 900306 27 0

John G. Bennett's Talks on
BEELZEBUB'S TALES
⑥

When Mr Bennett first read *All and Everything
Beelzebub's Tales to his Grandson* in 1948,
he was convinced that it would have a powerful
impact on all who came across it. With Gurdjieff's
approval he undertook a series of lectures in London preparing people to grasp the book's message.
When the book was published in 1950 there was
little response outside the small circle of those
already familiar with Gurdjieff's ideas. The world
was not yet ready. Since that time, and even more
so since the 1920's when the book was written, the
world has undergone great changes, especially in
attitudes of mind. Now it is easy in some sense or
other to accept that man is a machine, that the
planet is suffering an energy crisis, and that none
of the established modes of thought are adequate
to the human situation. Gurdjieff's book was
directed towards a world of accelerating complexity
and described where realistic hope for mankind
could be found. It is a treatise on psychology,
history, cosmology,ecology, sociology, art, science
religion and much that is unclassifiable.

Never claiming to be a true initiate capable of
unravelling and transmitting the essential meaning
of *Beelzebub's Tales,* Bennett nevertheless did
all that he could to give people access to the
book and its significance. Bennett regarded it as
a work of superhuman genius and containing
expressions of reality which by their very nature
were bound to make severe demands on any reader.
The talks collected in this monograph are represen-
tative of Bennett's expositions from 1949 to 1974.
There is no attempt to explain away and give easy
definitions of the complex and sometimes wonder-
fully barbarous expressions which Gurdjieff used.
Bennett gave people a spade to do their own dig-
ging with.

For those who have felt attraction to *Beelzebub's
Tales* these talks will be invaluable. They are at
present the only generally available commentaries
which attempt to understand the book in more than
a psychological way.

ISBN 0 900306 36 X

Needs of a New Age ⑦
Community

by J.G.Bennett

According to Bennett schools such as the Academy at Sherborne were only the first step in the work of creating a new way of life for people. The talks in this monograph are about steps to come. They do not provide a blueprint for what is needed but draw attention to what really matters. In order to live together differently the work must penetrate into the structure of our lives and particularly into our relationships with each other.

Included in this monograph is Bennett's interpretation of the Sermon on the Mount which he took to be a *legominism* directed towards those who would undertake the making of a New World.

ISBN 0 900306 47 5

IN PREPARATION